BAKE IT IN A CUP!

SIMPLE MEALS and SWEETS
KIDS CAN BAKE in SILICONE CUPS

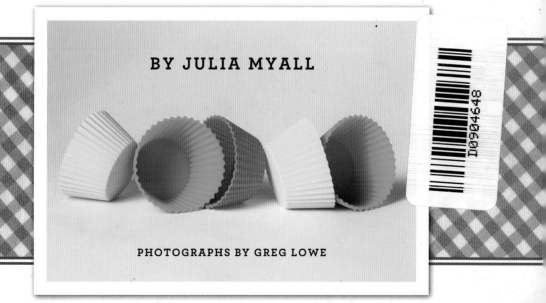

BY JULIA MYALL

PHOTOGRAPHS BY GREG LOWE

chronicle books · san francisco

To my mom and to my family, who have shown me
that a lot of love comes from the kitchen.
—JM

Text © 2012 by **JULIA MYALL.**

Photographs © 2012 by **CHRONICLE BOOKS.**

ISBN 978-1-4521-0877-3

Manufactured in China.

Book design by **TRACY SUNRIZE JOHNSON.**
Typeset in Archer and Burbank.

10 9 8 7 6 5 4 3 2 1

For ages 6 and up.

Kit materials conform to ASTM F963
and CPSIA 2008 safety standards.

Chronicle Books LLC
680 Second Street
San Francisco, California 94107

WWW.CHRONICLEKIDS.COM

TABLE OF CONTENTS

SUPER LITTLE SIDES

SWEET TREATS

TO THE BEST BAKER . . . YOU!

INTRODUCTION

FOR MORE THAN JUST CUPCAKES!

You are now the proud owner of six silicone cups! They're **FUN,** they're **FLEXIBLE,** and they come in **IRRESISTIBLE COLORS!** What can you do with them? When it comes to baking with your cups, the options are endless: You can make rice, bake desserts, poach an egg, and much more. The recipes in *Bake It in a Cup!* are just the beginning of the many baking adventures you will have with your cups!

These cups may look like cupcake holders, but silicone cups can be used for so much more! You can **BAKE, ROAST, MICROWAVE,** and **FREEZE** with them. Plus, since silicone is nonstick, you don't have to grease them and your recipes still slide out easily, making cleanup a snap (no standing over the sink trying to scrub 'em!).

Your new cups are **BENDABLE AND FLEXIBLE**—you can even turn them inside out! Peel back their sides to help get the food out, and turn them inside out to wash them. The cups are also **EASY TO HANDLE** after cooking, because they're cool to the touch within a few minutes of leaving the oven.

The recipes in *Bake It in a Cup!* are for meals, side dishes, snacks, and sweets. Each recipe has a short list of ingredients and should not take you very long to make. You can bake a quick snack for yourself, you can cook for a group of friends after school, or you can make the main course, side dish, or dessert for a family dinner. The recipes in this book will help you make an entire meal—from main course to dessert!

Use this cookbook to introduce yourself to **NEW FOODS AND TASTES.** You will also find out new ways to cook vegetables with great flavors, and you'll learn about new side dishes—like quinoa. You'll even find out how to make latkes—with zucchini! (Trust me—you'll want seconds!)

This cookbook packs all the key ingredients of **FUN IN THE KITCHEN.** Choose a recipe that strikes your fancy, grab your six cups and your ingredients, and let's get cooking!

USING YOUR CUPS

You are now the proud owner of six **COLORFUL, BENDABLE, WONDERFUL** silicone cups. Here are a few tips to keep in mind when you use them.

Wash 'em first.
Wash and dry your cups before using them the first time.

Beware of hot stuff.
Always use a hot pad or an oven mitt when handling cups that are fresh from the oven. Soon after cooking, the edges of the cup may be cool, but the part with the food in it will still be hot. So be careful! And don't forget about steam. All food releases steam when cooked, so watch out for hot steam when you're turning food out of your cups.

Stuck in the cup?
If something doesn't slide right out of the cup, give it more time to cool. Then try gently squeezing the base, using an oven mitt if the cup is still too warm to touch. Squeeze the base a few times in different spots, and then try to release the food again. If that doesn't help, slide a spoon or a butter knife between the edge of the cup and the food to help ease it out.

Clean up in a snap!
Cleaning your cups is easy. You can give them a quick wash with a soapy sponge in the sink, or you can put them in the top rack of the dishwasher.

KITCHEN SAFETY

You'll see this symbol  whenever a recipe step involves cutting with a sharp knife, using a kitchen appliance, or handling hot things. That's when you should **BE ESPECIALLY CAREFUL.** Ask for adult help whenever the step requires it or whenever you're doing something that's totally new to you.

Also, when an ingredient list calls for a pre-chopped item, ask an adult for help, especially if the item is tough to cut or if you're just not used to chopping. No matter what, an adult should be around whenever you're cooking, so you can get help any time you need it.

- PART 1 -

BREAKFAST IN A CUP

Poached Eggs

Use your cups to make eggs the easy way!

1 **egg**
1 **piece of bread (your choice)**
Butter
Pinch of **salt**
Pinch of **pepper**

1. Place one of your cups on a plate. Crack the egg into the cup.

2. Microwave the egg on high for 40 seconds.

3. Meanwhile, toast the bread.

4. Spread butter on the bread.

5. Remove the egg from the microwave, let it cool for 2 minutes, and then spoon out the egg onto the toast. ⚠

6. Add salt and pepper to taste.

TRY IT THIS WAY!

You can enjoy your poached egg plain, or you can add extras to the top of the egg after it's cooked, like turkey, cheese (your choice), chopped tomato, and bacon. You will need ¼ cup of each.

Crêpes

These thin pancakes are perfect to fill with savory or sweet options!

INGREDIENTS FOR 12 CRÊPES:

1 **egg**
1 teaspoon **granulated sugar**
½ teaspoon **salt**
½ cup **all-purpose flour**
¼ cup (½ stick) **unsalted butter**
1 cup **milk, at room temperature**
Pinch of **nutmeg**

1. Preheat the oven to 325°F.

2. Break the egg into a medium bowl.

3. Add the sugar, salt, and flour and whisk until the ingredients are well incorporated.

4. Melt the butter in the microwave on high for 10 to 15 seconds.

5. Add the butter to the egg mixture, and whisk until the batter is smooth.

6. Whisk in the milk and nutmeg.

7. Pour 1 tablespoon of the mixture into each cup.

8. Place the cups on a baking sheet, and bake for 15 minutes, or until golden. Allow to cool for 5 minutes. Repeat to make 6 more. ⚠

TRY IT THIS WAY!

For sweet crêpes, serve them with jelly or jam (your choice), Nutella, and whipped cream. For savory crêpes, consider chopped bacon, chives, and sour cream.

Granola Cups

Get a boost of energy from these granola cups, which are a great way to kick off your day—or to give you a pick-me-up in the afternoon!

INGREDIENTS FOR 6 BARS:

4 (whole) **graham crackers**
½ cup **rolled oats or oat-based cereal**
¼ cup **chocolate chips**
¼ cup **dried fruit**
1 tablespoon **flax seeds**
¼ cup **sweetened condensed milk**

1. Preheat the oven to 350°F.

2. Put the graham crackers in a zippered plastic bag, press out the air, and seal. Crush them with a rolling pin until they look like sand.

3. In a medium bowl, add the graham crackers, oats, chocolate chips, dried fruit, and flax seeds, and mix until the ingredients are well combined.

4. Pour in the condensed milk and mix again until well incorporated.

5. Place ¼ cup of granola into each cup.

6. Place the cups on a baking sheet. Bake for 20 minutes, or until golden. ⚠ Allow to cool for 5 minutes before enjoying.

Lemon-Yogurt Muffins

These muffins have just the right amount of lemon to wake you up
and to start your day off with zest!

INGREDIENTS FOR 12 MUFFINS:

MUFFINS
2 cups **all-purpose flour**
1 teaspoon **baking powder**
1 teaspoon **baking soda**
¼ teaspoon **salt**
1¼ cups **plain yogurt, at room temperature**
2 **eggs, at room temperature**
¼ cup (½ stick) **unsalted butter, melted
and cooled to room temperature**
¼ cup **granulated sugar**
2 tablespoons **honey**
1 tablespoon **lemon zest**

LEMON SYRUP
1 tablespoon **lemon juice**
⅓ cup **powdered sugar**
3 tablespoons **water**

TO MAKE THE MUFFINS

1. Preheat the oven to 350°F.

2. In a medium bowl, mix together the
flour, baking powder, baking soda, and salt.
Set aside.

3. In another medium bowl, mix together the yogurt, eggs, butter, sugar, honey, and lemon zest and beat well until combined.

4. Add the dry ingredients to the wet ingredients and mix until thoroughly combined.

5. Spoon half of the batter into the 6 cups, filling them two-thirds full.

6. Place the cups on a baking sheet and bake for 20 minutes, or until a butter knife or toothpick inserted into the center of a muffin comes out clean. ⚠

7. Let cool for 10 minutes, then gently peel away the cups.

8. Refill the cups to make 6 more muffins the same way.

TO MAKE THE SYRUP

Combine all of the ingredients in a bowl. Stir until well mixed, then pour an equal portion on top of each muffin.

Blueberry Blasters

Pop one of these flavorful muffins in your mouth, and you'll be bursting with energy!

INGREDIENTS FOR 12 MUFFINS:

1½ cups **all-purpose flour**
1 teaspoon **baking soda**
Pinch of **salt**
½ cup (1 stick) **unsalted butter**
1 cup **granulated sugar**
1 **egg, at room temperature**
1 teaspoon **vanilla extract**
¾ cup **milk**
1 cup **blueberries**

1. Preheat the oven to 350°F.

2. In a medium bowl, mix together the flour, baking soda, and salt.

3. In another medium bowl, combine the butter and sugar. Mix well with a fork until the mixture is creamy and smooth.

4. Add the egg and vanilla to the butter mixture, and mix until combined.

5. Slowly add the flour mixture to the butter mixture and stir with a fork until well combined.

6. Add the milk and mix until well incorporated. Then add the blueberries and lightly stir.

7. Spoon half of the batter into the 6 cups, filling them two-thirds full.

8. Place the cups on a baking sheet, and bake for 20 minutes, or until a butter knife or toothpick inserted into the center of a muffin comes out clean. ⚠

9. Let cool for 5 minutes, and then gently peel back the cups.

10. Refill the cups to make 6 more muffins the same way.

PART 2

MINI MAIN COURSES

Popcorn Shrimp

Pop these shrimp into your mouth for a healthful, quick, protein-packed snack,
or serve them with a super side as the main course!

INGREDIENTS FOR 6 SERVINGS:

18 pieces **raw medium-size shrimp,**
peeled and deveined

1 **egg**

¼ cup **milk**

½ cup **dry bread crumbs or crushed croutons**

1 teaspoon **chopped fresh parsley**

¼ teaspoon **garlic powder**

3 tablespoons **unsalted butter, diced**

1. Preheat the oven to 400°F.

2. Rinse the shrimp and drain them in a colander.

3. In a small bowl, whisk together the egg and milk and set aside.

4. In another small bowl, combine the bread crumbs or crushed croutons, parsley, and garlic powder. Stir with a fork until well mixed.

5. Place the cups on a baking sheet.

6. Take three of the shrimp and place them in the egg and milk mixture.

7. Next, take the same three shrimp out of the egg mixture and roll them in the bread crumb mixture.

8. Place the breaded shrimp in one of the cups. Repeat steps 6 through 8 for the remaining cups.

9. Place a pat (½ tablespoon) of butter on top of the shrimp in each cup.

10. Bake until golden brown, about 20 minutes.
Let cool for 10 minutes, then gently remove the shrimp.

Tamales

*Serve these melt-in-your-mouth cornmeal and chicken morsels
with some freshly sliced avocado, salsa, and sour cream, and you
will be treated to a fabulous meal!*

INGREDIENTS FOR 6 TAMALES:

½ cup (1 stick) **unsalted butter, at room
temperature,** plus 6 tablespoons
½ teaspoon **baking powder**
Pinch of **salt**
¾ cup **prepared fresh masa**
½ cup **all-purpose flour**
1 cup **chicken broth**
1 **cooked chicken breast, chopped into
bite-size pieces**
1 cup **store-bought salsa**
½ cup **corn kernels**

1. Preheat the oven to 375°F.

2. In a medium bowl, beat together the ½ cup
of butter, the baking powder, and salt with a fork
until creamy.

3. Add the masa and flour. Continue to beat till soft and fluffy.

4. Add the broth and mix until a soft batter forms. Set aside.

5. In another medium bowl, combine the chicken, salsa, and corn kernels. Lightly mix together with a fork.

6. Put a pat of butter (½ tablespoon) in the bottom of each cup.

7. Add a spoonful of the masa mixture to each cup. Then add a spoonful of the chicken mixture on top of each.

8. Add one more spoonful of masa mix to each cup, and another pat of butter on top of that. Use a spoon to pat down the mixture.

9. Place the cups on a baking sheet and place a square of aluminum foil securely on top of each cup.

10. Bake for 15 minutes. ⚠ With adult help, remove the baking sheet from the oven and remove the foil. Place the sheet back into the oven and bake for an additional 5 minutes, until the tamales look golden.

11. Let cool for 10 minutes, then gently peel away the cups and remove the tamales.

Chicken Roulades

"Roulade" comes from the French word rouler, which means "to roll."
These roulades are fun and easy to make. Serve with one of our super sides
for a hearty meal!

INGREDIENTS FOR 6 SERVINGS:

3 **boneless skinless chicken breasts**
6 ounces **cream cheese**
½ cup **dried cranberries**
1 teaspoon **finely chopped orange zest**
1 teaspoon **chopped parsley**
Pinch of **salt**
Pinch of **pepper**
3 tablespoons **unsalted butter**

1. Preheat the oven to 325°F.

2. Take 1 chicken breast and place it on a piece of plastic wrap.

3. With adult help, cut the chicken breast down the middle lengthwise like you are slicing a baguette. You now have two long pieces of chicken. ⚠

4. Place another piece of plastic wrap on top of the 2 pieces of chicken. Pound with a wooden spoon until the chicken is flattened to around ½ inch thick. Do the same with the other two breasts.

5. In a medium bowl, add the cream cheese, cranberries, orange zest, and parsley and blend until the ingredients are well combined.

6. Take one piece of chicken and spread 2 tablespoons of the cream cheese mixture down the middle. Do the same with the other five chicken pieces.

7. Then roll up each chicken piece to look like a snail.

8. Place one roll in each cup.

9. Sprinkle salt and pepper on top of each rolled chicken. Top off each roll with a pat (½ tablespoon) of butter.

10. Place the cups on a baking sheet and bake for 20 minutes, or until the tops are lightly golden. Let cool for 5 minutes, then remove the roulades from the cups and serve. ⚠

Tuna Casseroles

Casseroles combine lots of what you love, all in one place. In this recipe, take tuna and mix it together with scallions and parsley for a flavorful dish.

1 can (8 ounces) **water-packed tuna, drained**

2 cups **dry pasta (your choice; if using long pasta, break into 2-inch pieces)**

1 **tomato, finely diced**

¼ cup **chopped scallions**

1 **egg**

1 tablespoon **chopped parsley**

¼ teaspoon **balsamic vinegar**

1 cup **heavy whipping cream**

½ cup **bread crumbs**

3 tablespoons **unsalted butter**

1. Preheat the oven to 350°F.

2. In a medium bowl, combine the tuna, pasta, tomato, scallions, egg, parsley, and vinegar. Mix until the ingredients are well combined.

3. Place the cups on a baking sheet.

4. Spoon the mixture into each cup, filling the cups three-fourths full.

5. Pour equal amounts of cream into each cup.

6. Next, sprinkle the bread crumbs on top of each cup.

7. Finally, place a pat (½ tablespoon) of butter on top of the bread crumbs.

8. Bake for 20 minutes, or until the bread crumbs are golden. Let cool for 5 minutes before serving. ⚠

TRY IT THIS WAY!

If you prefer, use 8 ounces canned chicken instead of the tuna, and ½ cup chopped red peppers.

Calzones

You can have a lot of fun with this recipe: Toss the dough in the air like a real chef,
then fill your mini stuffed pizzas with any topping you like!

INGREDIENTS FOR 6 CALZONES

1½ teaspoons **active dry yeast**
1 teaspoon **honey**
¾ cup **warm water**
2¼ cups **all-purpose flour**
1 teaspoon **salt**
1 tablespoon **olive oil**
1½ cups of **your choice of filling:
cooked sausage, mozzarella cheese,
or chopped tomatoes and basil**

1. Preheat the oven to 400°F.

2. In a small bowl, combine the yeast, honey, and warm water and stir. Wait about 2 minutes for bubbles to appear (this means the yeast is active).

3. In a medium bowl, add the flour and salt.

4. Slowly pour the olive oil and the yeast mixture into the flour mixture. With adult help, use an electric mixer and mix on low speed until a ball of dough forms. ⚠

5. Transfer the dough to a floured countertop or cutting board, and roll out the dough to about ½-inch thick with a rolling pin.

6. Place a cup upside down on the dough and use a butter knife to cut around it. Repeat to make 12 disks total.

7. Place one dough disk inside each cup. Use your fingers to press the dough firmly into the bottom.

8. Add fillings to the center of each cup, making the cups three-fourths full.

9. Place a second dough disk on top of each cup to form the calzone. Press the edges of the dough disks together so that the bottom and top disks of dough are secured.

10. Place the cups on a baking sheet, and bake on the bottom oven rack for 20 minutes, or until the tops are lightly golden. Allow to cool for 10 minutes before serving. ⚠

Broccoli Casseroles

This is a great way to eat your vegetables! Mix in broccoli with pasta and cheese for an irresistible combination.

INGREDIENTS FOR 6 CASSEROLES:

2 cups **dry pasta (your choice)**
1⅓ cups **chopped broccoli**
1 **egg**
2 tablespoons **shredded mozzarella cheese**
1 tablespoon **grated Parmesan cheese**
¼ teaspoon **garlic salt**
1 cup **heavy whipping cream**
2 tablespoons **dry bread crumbs**
3 tablespoons **unsalted butter**

1. Preheat the oven to 350°F.

2. In a medium bowl, combine the pasta, broccoli, egg, mozzarella, Parmesan, and garlic salt.

3. Spoon the mixture into each cup, filling them three-fourths full.

4. Pour equal amounts of the cream into each cup.

5. Next, sprinkle the bread crumbs on top of each cup.

6. Finally, place a pat (½ tablespoon) of butter on top of the bread crumbs.

7. Place the cups on a baking sheet and bake for 20 minutes, or until the bread crumbs are golden. Let cool for 5 minutes before serving. ⚠

TRY IT THIS WAY!

To switch this up to a more meaty option, replace the broccoli with 1 cup cooked chicken or sausage.

For other veggie options, try 1 cup chopped zucchini, red peppers, or tomatoes.

Quinoa

This grain is often called a "super food" because it contains valuable nutrients. The best part? It also tastes great, especially when you add flavorful veggies to the mix. Serve this with any of the main courses for a side that has an extra bite!

INGREDIENTS FOR 6 CUPS:

1 medium **carrot, diced**
¼ **onion, chopped**
¼ cup **frozen peas**
1¾ cups **quinoa**
1¾ cups **chicken stock**
3 tablespoons **unsalted butter**
6 tablespoons **milk**

1. Preheat the oven to 375°F.

2. In a medium bowl, place the carrot, onion, and peas and mix until combined. Add the quinoa to the vegetable mixture and toss to combine.

3. Place a spoonful of the mixture in each cup, filling them three-fourths full.

4. Place the cups on a baking sheet.

5. Pour stock evenly over the quinoa. Place a pat of butter (½ tablespoon) on top of each cup. Bake for 10 minutes. ⚠

6. With adult help, remove the cups from the oven and add 1 tablespoon of milk to each cup. Stir lightly with a spoon. ⚠

7. Bake for 10 more minutes, or until tender. Let cool for 5 minutes before serving. ⚠

Baked Yams

Yams (sometimes called sweet potatoes) are surprisingly sweet—pair this side with an especially savory dish for a delicious balance of flavors.

INGREDIENTS FOR 6 CUPS:

¼ cup **water**

1 pound **red garnet yams, peeled and chopped into bite-sized pieces**

¼ teaspoon **ground nutmeg**

3 tablespoons **unsalted butter**

1 cup **mini marshmallows**

1. Preheat the oven to 350°F.

2. Pour an equal amount of water into the bottom of each cup.

3. In a medium bowl, place the yams and sprinkle in the nutmeg. Toss lightly to cover the yams with the nutmeg.

4. Spoon the yam mixture into each cup.

5. Place a pat (½ tablespoon) of butter on top of each cup.

6. Sprinkle the marshmallows on top.

7. Place the cups on a baking sheet and cover each with a piece of aluminum foil. Bake for 40 minutes and then, with adult help, remove the sheet from the oven and take the foil off of the cups. ⚠

8. Return the baking sheet and the cups to the oven for 20 minutes more, or until the marshmallows look golden. Let cool for 10 minutes before serving. ⚠

Brown Rice Poppers

Brown rice is not only good for you, it is tasty! These poppers go especially well with the Chicken Roulades (page 25). They are also delicious with your favorite steamed vegetables!

1. Preheat the oven to 350°F.

2. Place a pat (½ tablespoon) of butter in the bottom of each cup.

3. Pour rice into each cup, filling the cups one-fourth full.

4. Pour an equal amount of the water into each cup.

5. Place the cups on a baking sheet and cover each cup with foil.

6. Bake for 20 to 30 minutes, or until all the water is absorbed and the rice is tender. ⚠

7. Let cool for 5 minutes, then turn the rice out onto plates, if desired, for an eye-popping presentation. ⚠

Stuffed Peppers

Use your cups to hold these delicious stuffed peppers. Mozzarella cheese is suggested below, but you can also use your favorite cheese!

INGREDIENTS FOR 6 PEPPERS:

3 **red peppers, seeded and cut into six strips**
1 cup **white rice**
1 cup **store-bought salsa**
3 tablespoons **shredded mozzarella cheese**
2 cups **water**

1. Place 3 strips of pepper, cut-side up, in each cup.

2. In a small bowl, mix together the rice, salsa, and mozzarella.

3. Spoon the rice mixture into the center of the pepper strips.

4. Place the cups on a baking sheet.

5. Pour an equal amount of the water into each cup, filling each cup up to the top.

6. Place a sheet of foil over all six cups. Bake for 20 to 30 minutes, or until the tops are lightly golden. Let cool for 5 minutes before serving. ⚠

TRY IT THIS WAY!

Part of the fun of making stuffed peppers is to be creative about how they are filled. Here are some additional suggestions, but don't be afraid to mix and match your favorite foods!

1 CUP CHOPPED COOKED CHICKEN, SAUSAGE, OR BEEF

2 TABLESPOONS CHOPPED FRESH PARSLEY, BASIL, OR OREGANO

½ CUP BLUE CHEESE, CHEDDAR, OR GOAT CHEESE

1 CUP CHOPPED ZUCCHINI, TOMATOES, OR CORN

Latkes

These potato pancakes are usually served during Hannukah, but why not enjoy them year-round? They're that delicious! This recipe has a secret ingredient, zucchini, which adds an extra bite to that favorite taste.

INGREDIENTS FOR 12 LATKES:

1 medium **russet potato, peeled and grated**

1 medium **zucchini, peeled and grated**

¼ **onion, chopped**

1 tablespoon **all-purpose flour**

¼ teaspoon **baking powder**

Pinch of **salt**

Pinch of **pepper**

1 **egg, at room temperature**

6 tablespoons **unsalted butter**

Sour cream
Applesauce

1. Preheat the oven to 400°F.

2. Combine the potato, zucchini, onion, flour, baking powder, salt, and pepper in a medium bowl.

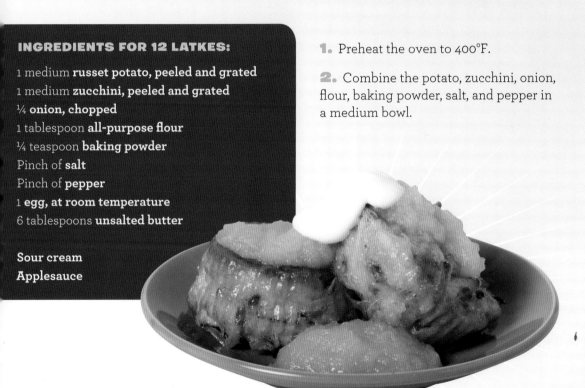

3. In a small bowl, crack the egg and whisk it with a fork until well beaten.

4. Pour the egg into the zucchini and potato mixture and mix until the ingredients are well combined.

5. Place the cups on a baking sheet.

6. Add ½ tablespoon of butter to each cup. Then, add 1 tablespoon of the potato mixture to each cup.

7. Bake for 15 minutes, and then remove from the oven.

8. With an adult's help, use a fork to flip the latke in each cup. Return to the oven and bake another 15 minutes, or until golden. ⚠

9. Repeat to make more latkes in the same way.

10. Serve with sour cream and applesauce.

Twice-Baked Potatoes

Baking these potatoes twice ensures they're cooked through—and have the perfect texture! Top 'em off with sour cream, or serve with the old standard: ketchup.

INGREDIENTS FOR 6 CUPS:

3 **baking potatoes**
½ cup **heavy whipping cream**
¾ cup **bacon bits**
¾ cup **shredded Cheddar cheese**
6 tablespoons **unsalted butter, cut into pieces**
1 tablespoon **chopped scallions**
Pinch of **salt**
Pinch of **pepper**

1. Preheat the oven to 350°F.

2. With adult help, rinse off the outside of each potato and use a fork to poke holes in it. ⚠

3. Place the potatoes on a baking sheet.

4. Bake the potatoes on the middle oven rack for 1 hour (some potatoes may need slightly more time, depending on the size), or until a fork inserted into the potato goes in easily. ⚠

5. With adult help, remove the potatoes from the oven and let cool for 1 hour. ⚠

6. With adult help, slice the potatoes in half widthwise and scoop the insides out into a small bowl. Set the skins aside for use in step 10. ⚠

7. Using a fork, mash the potato insides until no large lumps remain.

8. In another small bowl, whip the whipping cream using an electric mixer until soft peaks form. ⚠

9. Add the bacon, cheese, butter, scallions, salt, pepper, and the whipped cream to the mashed potatoes, and mix until well combined.

10. Place one reserved potato skin in each cup and fill with the mashed potato mixture.

11. Bake for 15 to 20 minutes, or until lightly golden brown on top. Cool for 5 minutes, then serve in the cups, or scoop out onto plates. ⚠

Cheese Biscuits

These light and cheesy biscuits will add flavor to any meal.

INGREDIENTS FOR 12 BISCUITS:

1 cup **bread flour or all-purpose flour**
2 teaspoons **baking powder**
¼ teaspoon **baking soda**
⅓ cup **butter**
½ cup **shredded Cheddar cheese**
¾ cup **buttermilk**

1. Preheat the oven to 450°F.

2. In a medium bowl, sift together the flour, baking powder, and baking soda.

3. Cut the butter into pea-size pieces and add to the bowl.

4. Using your hands, mix together the butter and dry ingredients until they are well combined.

5. Add the cheese to the butter mixture and stir with a spoon until the ingredients are well incorporated.

6. Add the buttermilk and stir just until blended.

7. Sprinkle some extra flour on the counter-top and, with a rolling pin, roll out the dough to a ½-inch thickness.

8. Place a cup upside down on the dough and use a butter knife to cut around it. Repeat to make 12 rounds total.

9. If baking 6 biscuits at a time, put a dough piece in each cup and place the cups on a baking sheet. If you are baking all 12 biscuits without using cups, place the rounds on a greased baking sheet.

10. Bake for 10 to 15 minutes, or until lightly browned. Let cool for 5 minutes before serving. ⚠

11. If using the cups, repeat steps 9 and 10 for the remaining dough.

Hot Lava Cakes

We challenge you to eat these cakes and not make a mess!
The chocolatey gooiness is part of the fun!

INGREDIENTS FOR 6 CAKES:

1 cup **all-purpose flour**
¼ cup **granulated sugar**
2 teaspoons **baking powder**
¼ teaspoon **salt**
½ cup **chocolate chips**
1 cup (2 sticks) **unsalted butter**
⅓ cup **milk**
1 **egg yolk**
1 teaspoon **vanilla extract**

1 package **hot cocoa mix** or 1 tablespoon **cocoa powder** and 2 tablespoons **sugar**
1½ cups **hot water**

1. Preheat the oven to 325°F.

2. In a medium bowl, mix together the flour, sugar, baking powder, and salt.

3. In a microwavable bowl, place the chocolate chips and butter and microwave on high for 20 to 30 seconds, or until fully melted. ⚠

4. Add the melted chocolate and butter to the flour and mix well.

5. Add the milk, egg yolk, and vanilla to the chocolate batter.

6. Spoon the batter into each cup, filling each three-fourths full.

7. In a separate bowl, combine the cocoa mix and hot water and blend well.

8. Place the cups on a baking sheet. Then, pour the hot cocoa into each cup.

9. Bake for 20 minutes. Allow to cool for 5 to 10 minutes before serving. ⚠

Pecan Pies

You can serve these little pies for an after-dinner treat with ice cream or as a snack in your lunch.

INGREDIENTS FOR 6 PIES:

CRUST

½ cup (1 stick) **unsalted butter**

¼ cup **powdered sugar**

1 cup **all-purpose flour**

2 tablespoons **heavy whipping cream**

FILLING

1 cup **dark corn syrup**

½ cup **granulated sugar**

2 **eggs**

½ teaspoon **vanilla extract**

1 tablespoon **butter, melted**

Pinch of **salt**

½ cup **chopped pecans**

¼ cup **chocolate chips**

TO MAKE THE CRUST

1. Using a food processor (with adult help), combine the butter, powdered sugar, and flour and process on medium high until large crumbs form. ⚠

2. Add the cream and process for 2 more minutes, or just until the dough comes together in a rough ball. ⚠

3. Place 2 tablespoons of the dough into each cup. Press the dough evenly into the bottom and up the sides of each cup to form a crust.

4. Place the cups in the freezer to chill for 10 minutes. This helps firm up the dough so it will keep its shape better when you bake it.

TO MAKE THE FILLING

1. Preheat the oven to 350°F.

2. In a medium bowl, combine the corn syrup, granulated sugar, eggs, and vanilla until well mixed.

3. Add the melted butter and salt and continue to whisk until combined.

4. Divide the pecans and chocolate chips among the crust-filled cups. Pour an equal amount of the syrup mixture into each cup.

5. Place the cups on a baking sheet and bake for 25 minutes, or until the filling has set. Cool for 10 minutes before serving. ⚠

Cream Puffs

Serve these sweet, delicate little puffs topped with chocolate sauce or fresh strawberries!

INGREDIENTS FOR 6 PUFFS:

2 **eggs**
½ cup **water**
¼ cup (½ stick) **unsalted butter**
½ cup **all-purpose flour**
1 tablespoon **granulated sugar**
Pinch of **salt**
2 cups **whipped cream**
3 **strawberries, halved**

1. Preheat the oven to 375°F.

2. In a medium bowl and with adult help, beat the eggs with an electric mixer on high until they appear pale yellow in color. Set aside.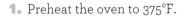

3. Put the water and butter in a saucepan and bring to a boil. Turn off the heat. ⚠

4. In a medium bowl, sift together the flour, sugar, and salt.

5. Add the dry ingredients to the water and butter and stir the mixture until a ball of dough forms.

6. Place the dough ball in a medium bowl. Using an electric mixer (with adult help), mix the dough on low for 5 minutes, or until the mixture has cooled to room temperature. ⚠

7. Add the eggs to the ball of dough and continue to mix on low until the dough is sticky.

8. With a spoon, scoop the mixture into the cups, filling each one three-fourths full.

9. Place the cups on a baking sheet and bake for 30 minutes, then turn off the oven and let the cups remain there for another 15 minutes. ⚠

10. Remove from the oven and let cool for 10 minutes. ⚠

11. Remove the puffs from the cups by using a spatula to carefully loosen them from the sides of the cups.

12. Cut each puff in half, fill the bottom of the puff with whipped cream, then gently replace top. ⚠

13. Top each puff with a halved strawberry.

Cheesecake

These mini cheesecakes have a creamy filling and a crust that has a satisfying crunch!

INGREDIENTS FOR 6 CHEESECAKES:

CRUST
9 whole **graham crackers**
⅓ cup **granulated sugar**
½ cup (1 stick) **unsalted butter, melted and cooled**

FILLING
1 pound **cream cheese, at room temperature**
2 **eggs**
¼ cup **granulated sugar**
1 teaspoon **vanilla extract**

TO MAKE THE CRUST

1. Put the graham crackers and the sugar in a zippered plastic bag, press out the air, and seal. Crush them with a rolling pin until they look like sand.

2. Pour the graham cracker mixture into a medium bowl. Add the butter and mix together with a fork until the graham cracker crumbs are completely coated.

3. Place 2 tablespoons of the crust mixture into each cup and press down with the back of a spoon. Press the mixture down with your fingers to form an even disk in the bottom of each cup.

4. Place the cups on a baking sheet.

TO MAKE THE FILLING

1. Preheat the oven to 350°F.

2. In a bowl and using an electric mixer (with adult help) on high, beat together the cream cheese, eggs, sugar, and vanilla for 2 minutes, or until well blended. ⚠

3. Use a spoon to fill each cup three-fourths full with the cream cheese filling.

4. Bake for 30 minutes, until the filling has set. Refrigerate until chilled for at least 1 hour before serving. ⚠

Fruit Cobbler

Fill these cobblers with your favorite fruit. Try fresh berries, like strawberries or blueberries, or use a stone fruit, like peaches or plums. No matter how this cobbler crumbles, you'll love it!

INGREDIENTS FOR 6 COBBLERS:

FILLING

3 cups **berries (your choice), washed**

⅓ cup **granulated sugar**

¼ cup **molasses**

2 tablespoons **lemon juice**

¼ teaspoon **ground cinnamon**

¼ teaspoon **ground nutmeg**

¼ teaspoon **ground cloves**

CRUMBLE TOPPING

1 cup **all-purpose flour**

1½ teaspoons **baking powder**

¼ teaspoon **salt**

¼ cup (½ stick) **unsalted butter**

1 **egg**

⅓ cup **milk or heavy whipping cream**

TO MAKE THE FILLING

1. Preheat the oven to 425°F.

2. In a medium bowl, combine the berries, sugar, molasses, lemon juice, cinnamon, nutmeg, and cloves and stir until the ingredients are well combined.

3. Place the cups on a baking sheet. Spoon an equal amount of the mixture into each cup.

TO MAKE THE TOPPING

1. In a medium bowl, combine the flour, baking powder, and salt and stir with a fork to mix.

2. Add the butter, egg, and milk, and continue to stir until the mixture resembles large pebbles.

3. Spoon the mixture evenly over the berries in the cups.

4. Bake for 20 minutes, or until the tops are lightly golden. Cool for 15 minutes before serving. ⚠

5. Eat the cobbler out of the cups, or spoon out onto a plate and serve with ice cream.

Fruit Roll-Ups

This recipe takes simple to a whole new level: It only takes three ingredients to make this treat! A bonus is that these fruity goodies are packed with lots of vitamins, but they're so sweet, you'd never know it!

INGREDIENTS FOR 6 FRUIT ROLL-UPS:

8 ounces **fruit of your choice, like strawberries, raspberries, or blackberries, chopped into small pieces**

2 tablespoons **water**

¼ cup **honey**

1. Preheat the oven to 275°F.

2. With adult help, put the chopped fruit and water into a small pot. Cook over medium-high heat until the mixture boils, then reduce the heat to low and simmer for 5 minutes more. ⚠

3. Remove from the heat and let cool for 10 minutes.

4. With adult help, pour the mixture into a blender or food processor and puree for 2 minutes, or until the mixture is smooth. ⚠

5. Add the honey and continue to mix well.

6. Place the cups on a baking sheet and pour 1 tablespoon of puree into each cup.

7. Bake for 40 minutes, or until the fruit looks leathery. ⚠

8. Turn off the oven and leave the door closed. The cups should remain in the oven for an additional 8 to 10 hours (until the fruit dries).

9. When cooled and dry, peel the cups away from the fruit and enjoy immediately, or place in an airtight container for up to 14 days.

Madeleines

These little cakes are perfect to serve as a snack, dessert, or a sweet something with tea! Eat them at any time of day and you'll notice that they will put a smile on your face.

INGREDIENTS FOR 6 MADELEINES

1 cup **powdered sugar**
¼ cup plus 2 tablespoons **almond meal**
⅓ cup **all-purpose flour**
4 **egg whites**
⅓ cup **unsalted butter, melted**
1½ teaspoons **honey**
Pinch of **lemon zest**

1. Preheat the oven to 400°F.

2. In a medium bowl, mix together the sugar, almond meal, and flour.

3. Add the egg whites, one at a time, to the dry ingredients, whisking thoroughly after each addition. Add the melted butter to the mixture. Stir until the ingredients are well combined.

4. Stir the honey and zest into the mixture.

5. Spoon 2 tablespoons of the batter into each cup, filling each three-fourths full.

6. Place the cups on a baking sheet and bake for 30 minutes, or until a toothpick inserted into the center of one of the madeleines comes out clean. Let cool for 10 minutes before serving. ⚠

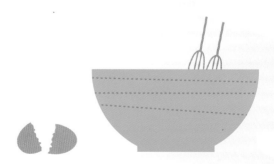

TO THE BEST BAKER... YOU!

BAKING A DISH—whether it's a main course, a snack, or a sweet treat—and then **SHARING IT WITH THE PEOPLE YOU LOVE,** makes you feel so good! I hope you have enjoyed baking the many recipes in this book and discovering new ways to make some of your favorite foods. Enjoy your new silicone cups, and continue to have **EXCITING—AND DELICIOUS—ADVENTURES IN THE KITCHEN!**

ABOUT THE AUTHOR

JULIA MYALL has worked as a chef in many premier San Francisco restaurants and as a cooking teacher at the American Embassy in Paris. She is the author of *Cook It in a Cup!* and *Party in a Cup!* She lives in Lafayette, California, with her husband and three children.

TABLE OF EQUIVALENTS

The exact equivalents in the following tables have been rounded for convenience.

LIQUID/DRY MEASUREMENTS

U.S.	METRIC
¼ teaspoon	1.25 milliliters
½ teaspoon	2.5 milliliters
1 teaspoon	5 milliliters
1 tablespoon (3 teaspoons)	15 milliliters
1 fluid ounce (2 tablespoons)	30 milliliters
¼ cup	60 milliliters
⅓ cup	80 milliliters
½ cup	120 milliliters
1 cup	240 milliliters
1 pint (2 cups)	480 milliliters
1 quart (4 cups, 32 ounces)	960 milliliters
1 gallon (4 quarts)	3.84 liters
1 ounce (by weight)	28 grams
1 pound	448 grams
2.2 pounds	1 kilogram

LENGTHS

U.S.	METRIC
⅛ inch	3 millimeters
¼ inch	6 millimeters
½ inch	12 millimeters
1 inch	2.5 centimeters

OVEN TEMPERATURE

FAHRENHEIT	CELSIUS	GAS
250	120	½
275	140	1
300	150	2
325	160	3
350	180	4
375	190	5
400	200	6
425	220	7
450	230	8
475	240	9
500	260	10